T0033446

A HISTORY OF MUSIC

FOR CHILDREN

MARY RICHARDS &
DAVID SCHWEITZER

A HISTORY OF MUSIC

FOR CHILDREN

ILLUSTRATED BY Rose Blake

CONTENTS

INTRODUCTION

Hello and welcome to a world of music! Before we get started, a few notes about the way this book is arranged. You'll see it's called a "history," but it's not divided up by dates or written in chronological order. That's because we're not telling a single story from start to finish. Instead, we'll jump around in time discovering different people, instruments and ways of making music as we go. We'll also look at some big questions: What is music and why do we make it? How has music been used through history? Why does it make us feel certain emotions?

From *Bach* to *Billie Eilish*, *Hildegard of Bingen* to *DJ Kool Herc*, *Mozart* to *Miriam Makeba*, our musicians come from many different times and places, but they all share a love of creating and playing music. As you're reading, you will know at what point in history the musicians were alive because we've included their birth dates in brackets. You'll also see our illustrator, Rose Blake, hopping through the pages—joining in with the music-making and meeting our musicians.

I'm Mary and I'm one of the authors of this book. I play the violin and I love writing about music, as well as art.

My name is David and I'm a composer for film and TV. I play many instruments and, together with Mary, I run a school orchestra.

Just as there's no single style of music, there's no one way to start listening to music either. We've created a playlist that features some of the music mentioned in this book. On page 92, you'll find a QR code that will take you to the online playlist, as well as some tips on ways to discover other music. What we've suggested is just a starting point—there's so much more you can explore for yourself! Listen to the music all around you—at home, at school and with your friends. Search out different examples, and make notes and playlists of what you like. You might end up making music yourself, or writing about the music makers you admire. Although many musicians spend years training, practicing and learning very special skills (such as ways of controlling their voices, or playing a particular instrument), everyone can enjoy music. We all hear music all the time. We all appreciate it. We can all join in.

I'm Rose and I'm the illustrator of this book. I belong to a choir in London and love listening to music whenever I'm drawing.

Follow us— your musical journey starts here!

The first musicians

Let's think back thousands of years. We can imagine our ancient ancestors waking up to the shrieks of birds in the treetops— and copying those sounds themselves. Birds, the original musicians, were singing their songs millions of years before humans lived on Earth. From the African savanna to the Amazon rainforest, birds everywhere start the day by singing a dawn chorus. This musical alarm clock tells us that the sun is rising.

Like us, birds sing different notes and rhythms, which together make tunes. Groups of birds sing together, and some birds even duet—when one calls out with a melody, its friend replies with another. But unlike humans, birds don't really sing for pleasure—even though we might like to imagine that they do. They make sounds to let other birds know where they are, to show off and attract mates, or to warn of nearby danger.

We humans, however, do create new music—or compose—for pleasure. As we'll discover in this book, besides using our voices we have invented thousands of instruments in all shapes and sizes. We've made instruments from wood, bone, metal, plastic and now computers. With these, we're able to express ourselves using sounds and tunes as well as words. We've also explored different ways of writing, performing and recording music. Let's take a journey and discover some amazing music that's been made—and the people who created it!

Inspired by birdsong

In his song *Three Little Birds*, musician **Bob Marley** (1945–1981) describes birds on his doorstep singing "melodies pure and true" and bringing him a hopeful message: "Don't worry about a thing!" Musicians across time have often been inspired by birds. One of the earliest songs written for choir in 13th-century England was about the sound of a cuckoo. This bird's familiar two-note call can also be heard in music by composers **Ludwig van Beethoven** (c. 1770–1827) and **Camille Saint-Saëns** (1835–1921).

In 1921, American composer **Amy Beach** (1867–1944) heard a hermit thrush singing outside her studio. She worked the bird's tune into a pair of pieces for piano. French composer **Olivier Messiaen** (1908–1992) was also fascinated by birdsong, and noted down birdcalls from all over the world. His wife, pianist **Yvonne Loriod** (1924–2010), told the story of walking in the woods and hearing the call of a curlew, which she recognized from Messiaen's music.

It's not just bird sounds that inspire musicians. Russian composer *Pyotr Tchaikovsky* (1840–1893) wrote the ballet *Swan Lake* in 1875. A ballet is a story told entirely through music and dance. The music of *Swan Lake* expresses the swans' graceful movements. Ballerinas, wearing tutus that look like feathers, glide across the stage like the birds on the lake in the story—which tells of a princess under a magic spell who is a swan by day and a human by night.

Next time you're walking in a park, listen to the sounds of nature all around you—they might just inspire a piece of music.

Jazz musician *Charlie Parker* (1920–1955), who played the saxophone, was given the nickname "Bird," and many of his best-known compositions had bird-related names, like *Bird Gets the Worm*. The famous New York jazz club Birdland that opened in 1949 was named after him.

The first instruments

So how did we begin making music—and why?

In ancient times, music would have been used for many different reasons. The first instrument was the human voice. The soft voices of parents have soothed babies to sleep for thousands of years.

Singing and making music together may have helped our ancestors to feel part of a group. Perhaps they sang certain tunes to show they belonged to a particular tribe or religion. They'd also sing to get excited before a battle, or to celebrate a victory. Rhythmic chants and marking time with a regular beat help people to dance, march or row in time with each other. Learning the same songs connects you with your friends—it's fun to sing together!

In ancient caves or buried deep underground, archaeologists have discovered the remains of instruments dating from 40,000 years ago. Early flutes were made from the bones of birds and animals, while drums and shakers were made from sticks, shells, seeds, pods and stones. Animal skins could also be dried and stretched to make drums. When humans discovered how to mold metal, other instruments with a whole new range of sounds were created.

Whatever the instrument, whatever the time or place, we can imagine people in the past celebrating with music just as we do today. Music helps us to connect with each other. In the words of American singer *Ella Fitzgerald* (1917–1996):

Music is the universal language— it brings people closer together.

THINKING ABOUT... *Sound and music*

"What's that racket? That's not music!" Have your adults
ever said something like this when they've heard the music you've
been listening to? Of course, what they really mean is, "I don't like
that sound—it's not to my taste." But when is something just sound
and when is it music? This can be a surprisingly difficult question
to answer!

It's not as easy as saying that music has a melody. Plenty of music
around the world is made using percussive instruments, with no tune
at all. Listen to a djembe ensemble from Guinea in West Africa, and
there can be no doubt that what they are playing is music, even
though there is no melody as such.

When Beethoven's *Grosse Fuge* was first
performed in 1825 it was reported that
it "sounded like noise" to his audience.

If you hear someone hammering a nail into a wall, you would think of it as a noise—and quite an annoying one! But if they were to start hammering a regular, repeating rhythm, within a few seconds your brain would start expecting the same pattern to carry on; you might even start tapping your foot or bobbing your head along. But has that sound become music? Probably not! Even though it has a repeating rhythm, a ticking clock is not music, nor is the regular drip of a tap that hasn't been fully turned off.

One possible answer to the question is that sound becomes music when the performer thinks of it as music, or when the listener hears it as music. Just as all pieces of music are different, so are all listeners. We all have our own ideas about what makes a good piece of music, just as we all enjoy particular sounds, tunes and rhythms.

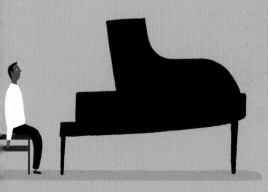

In 1952, *John Cage* (1912–1992) wrote a piece of music called 4'33", where the players performing were told to stay completely silent for four minutes and thirty-three seconds. The audience in the concert hall had to listen to the silence as if it was a musical performance. This is considered to be one of the most important musical works of the 20th century because it makes us ask the question, "What is music?" Cage said of the performance, "There's no such thing as silence. What they thought was silence, because they didn't know how to listen, was full of accidental sounds."

EXPLORING MUSIC
What music has been made in different times and places?

I'm Hildegard of Bingen. In the 12th century in Germany I was the head of a group of nuns. I wrote about religion and science, and composed songs, hymns and a musical play.

Ancient music

The history of music is a story of people and the different times and places they lived in. We know that music was important in the past, because the remains of early instruments still survive today. Musicians also appear in old paintings and sculpture—like these two ancient Egyptian players on the wall of the tomb of Rekhmire 3,000 years ago. However, we have to imagine the sounds that these early musicians were making! The music itself wasn't recorded or written down in a way that we can understand.

Wall painting of women playing the harp and lute, Egypt, 13th century BCE

Ancient stories also tell of music and musicians. According to Chinese legend, *Ling Lun* created a set of bamboo pipes, which he tuned to the call of the mythical phoenix. These notes are still used in the Chinese pentatonic, or five-tone, scale. For the ancient Greeks, music was linked to maths and astronomy—and also to their gods. In fact, the word music comes from the Muses—the nine Greek goddesses of knowledge. In one famous tale, two gods challenged each other to a musical duel. Pan played a kind of flute, and Apollo played a lyre made from a tortoise shell. Apollo was declared the winner. When Pan's follower, King Midas, dared to challenge the result, a furious Apollo punished him by changing his ears into those of a donkey.

Many sacred texts are full of stories about music. In the Bible, King David (best known as the boy who defeated the giant Goliath), was said to play the harp so sweetly that he was able to ward off evil spirits with his music. This story is mentioned in the song *Hallelujah*, written by **Leonard Cohen** (1934–2016).

Leonard, what was the secret chord?

A minor!

Baa-allelujah!

21

Music of the gods

Music can strongly affect the way we feel, so it isn't surprising that music has been closely linked with religion for such a long time.

Before writing was invented, and thousands of years before people could read, we learned songs by ear, or by listening. Religions around the world developed ceremonies to celebrate and honor their god or gods, and these often involved music. Prayers and stories could be passed on from generation to generation using songs and chants. The Islamic call to prayer, *adhan*, still rings out from the tallest point of mosques around the world, summoning people to pray. Other religious music involves songs for many singers, all performing different parts.

When *Hildegard of Bingen* was alive (c. 1098–1179), church musicians wrote simple lines of music that were easy to remember. They were sung in Latin, with no instruments accompanying them. Around this time, composers began to work out ways of writing music down. When music could be read, they were able to write more complicated parts, and introduce tunes to be sung by different voices at the same time. Hildegard wasn't famous in her lifetime, but her music lives on thanks to these early manuscripts.

Our brains release "feel good" chemicals when we sing together, and that makes the emotions we have even more powerful. Gospel music has its origins in the spiritual songs sung by Africans who were captured and forced to work as slaves in the American South in the 17th, 18th and 19th centuries. In these tunes, singers join in through call and response, where a line sung by one person is repeated by everyone else. Today, gospel music is performed around the world— and not just in churches. Artists *Aretha Franklin* (1942–2018) and *Tina Turner* (b. 1939) launched their careers singing gospel songs.

Music and power

For thousands of years, emperors, kings, queens, shahs and other rulers in history have used music to show their wealth and power. The musicians who filled the royal courts of China's Tang Dynasty in the 7th–9th centuries or the villas of the Medici family in 16th-century Florence performed on the finest instruments of their time. Musicians like *Wolfgang Amadeus Mozart* (1756–1791) were paid, or commissioned, to compose new works in honor of their powerful patrons. With his sister *Maria Anna* (1751–1829), Wolfgang traveled across Europe to perform in grand houses and palaces.

In 1717, German composer *George Frideric Handel* (1685–1759) wrote his *Water Music* for King George I of England. It was performed by musicians playing on boats as the King sailed up the River Thames. Not to be outdone, his son George II commissioned Handel to write *Music for the Royal Fireworks* in 1749, to celebrate the end of a war. People flocked to see it performed, causing one of the first recorded traffic jams, as horses and carriages were stuck on London Bridge for three hours!

In the 19th and 20th centuries many composers wrote music to show pride in their nations. Musicians including *Modest Mussorgsky* (1839–1881) in Russia, *Manuel de Falla* (1876–1946) in Spain and *Jean Sibelius* (1865–1957) in Finland, were inspired by the folk music of their countries. *Bedrich Smetana* (1824–1884) included a Czech dance called a polka in *Ma Vlast* (*My Country*), a work celebrating the beauty of his homeland. Smetana conjures up a musical picture of this ancient land, with its mighty river weaving through woods and fields, past villages and castles.

Music to entertain

What do you expect of a musical entertainer? To be wowed by their stage presence or astonished by their amazing skills? For thousands of years, all around the world, people have gathered to watch incredible performers.

From the late 11th century in Europe, musicians known as troubadours traveled around singing love poems or verses they'd written. They often accompanied themselves on harps or lutes. Around the same time in West Africa, performers called griots entertained and informed communities, singing tales of important events and traditions. These musicians—playing the kora, balafon or ngoni— are born into the job, which they pass on to their children. Many African griots today are descended from a long line of entertainers. *Toumani Diabaté* (b. 1965) from Mali, who plays the kora with his son Sidiki, is able to trace his musical ancestors over 70 generations!

KORA BALAFON NGONI

Concerts as we know them didn't really exist until the 18th century, a time when many concert halls were built. This changed the way music was performed. Instead of musicians playing in the background at a party, or a band playing in the open air, the singer, soloist or orchestra was now put on a stage. Today we associate classical concerts with people sitting quietly, concentrating on every note. But this wasn't always the case! Early audiences talked and clapped during and between pieces of music—sometimes drowning out the sound of the musicians altogether.

THEODOR HOSEMANN *Cartoon of Liszt and his admirers*, 1842

Like a modern-day pop star, Hungarian composer and pianist *Franz Liszt* (1811–1886) dazzled his audiences. There are stories of people fainting during his concerts, with some fans even taking cuttings of his hair!

THINKING ABOUT...Opera

In many times and places humans have told stories using music and song. From around 500 BCE, the ancient Greeks built open-air theaters to stage their plays, which often included singing and musical performers. Opera combines music, words, movement, scenery and costumes. It can be traced back to the 4th century in China, where stories and legends set to music were performed by actors in elaborate costumes and make-up. In Beijing Opera, the masks or face paint worn by the actors give the audience a clue to their characters—for example, white masks represent villains, while red stands for bravery and loyalty.

Opera as we know it today burst onto the scene in the 17th century in Italy (opera means "work" in Italian). Solo performers sang songs called *arias* that are full of feeling. Audiences connected to the emotions of the characters, who sang about love or tragedy. The first operas—such as *L'Orfeo* by **Claudio Monteverdi** (c. 1567–1643)—were performed for a private audience. But opera soon drew huge crowds to newly built opera houses.

With time, operas became more ambitious with bigger orchestras, complicated costumes and sets, and spectacular effects. Operas also got longer: the *Ring Cycle* by German composer **Richard Wagner** (1813–1883) lasted for 17 hours and was performed over four days! It told the Norse legend of a ring that gave its owner power over the whole world. If that sounds familiar, it definitely influenced **J.R.R. Tolkien** (1892–1973) when he wrote his book *The Lord of the Rings*.

Opera created superstars. Greek singer **Maria Callas** (1923–1977) rose to fame on Italian stages in Venice and Milan before her career took her all over the world. She was famous for her dramatic performances.

29

Music for everyone, everywhere

These days, we are never far from music—it's on TV, it's in the background when we go shopping and we can listen to almost anything on demand 24 hours a day. But until 100 years ago, it wasn't so easy to hear music. You might hear it in church or at a concert; if you were lucky enough to own an instrument, you might gather to make music with friends. But you wouldn't hear music in most places.

Recorded music changed all that. The invention of radio and records meant that music was heard by large audiences. For the first time, pop (short for "popular") musicians like *Elvis Presley* (1935–1977) or *Chuck Berry* (1926–2017) became famous not just in their home countries, but all over the world. On a trip to India in 1966, The Beatles guitarist *George Harrison* (1943–2001) learned to play the sitar from *Ravi Shankar* (1920–2012) and used it on the best-selling album, *Sgt. Pepper's Lonely Hearts Club Band*. This brought the sound of classical Indian music into millions of homes outside India for the first time.

Other inventions of the 20th century, like electric guitars and synthesizers, changed the way music sounded, too. New music was even made from old recordings. In the 1970s, *DJ Kool Herc* (b. 1955) —playing records at parties and on the streets of New York—took a beat or break from one part of a song, repeated it, and turned it into a new piece of music. Performers then rapped over the top. Soon, people were listening to recordings or mixtapes of the new sounds that DJs like Herc had created. This was the beginning of hip hop.

It's unlikely that Hildegarde or Mozart heard music from Asia, Africa or South America during their lives. But today, on our tablets, computers and smartphones, we are just one Internet search away from listening to music made at opposite ends of the Earth.

3

CREATING MUSIC
What do we use to make music?

I'm Jimi Hendrix, and I was born in the U.S. in 1942. I wowed the world with my electric guitar playing.

Voices

Our voices are incredible instruments. We can use them to sing solo, where we produce just one note at a time, or to sing with others, so our voices blend together. We can all sing the same tune in unison or we can sing different notes, creating harmonies.

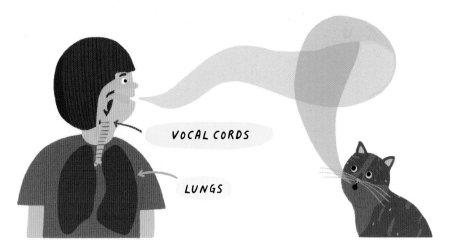

VOCAL CORDS

LUNGS

So how do voices work? When we speak or sing, we send air from our lungs through a delicate group of muscles in our throat called vocal cords, and out of our mouths. Different techniques can be used to change the sound of our voice. One style, ululation, involves moving the tongue up and down very fast while singing the note. It's often used by singers in North Africa and the Middle East to express powerful emotions. Another technique—*vibrato*, used by opera singers—is created by producing tiny vibrations in the vocal cords. In the art of Mongolian throat singing, singers produce two different pitches at once by creating an extra note called a harmonic.

ULULATION

VIBRATO

MONGOLIAN THROAT SINGING

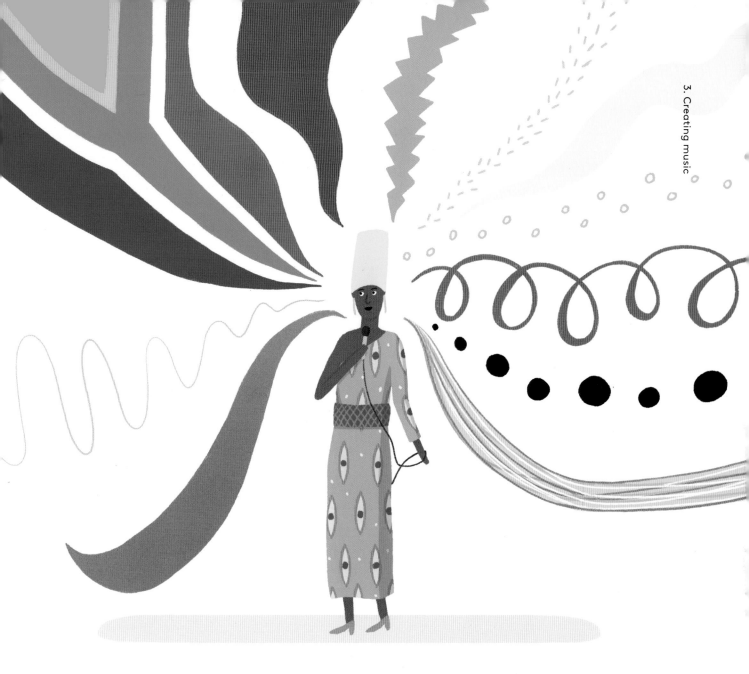

South African singer *Miriam Makeba* (1932–2008) became world
famous in the 1960s for the many different sounds she could create
with her voice. She sang in whispers, shouts and roars, often using
the *mbube* vocal harmonies sung by Zulu people, and the clicks
of her native Xhosa language. Makeba used her distinctive voice
and her influence to speak up against apartheid in South Africa,
campaigning for equality for Black South Africans who, for many
years, did not have the same rights as white citizens.

Voices improve with practice! The best way to learn to sing well is by
joining in with others, listening to lots of different styles and copying
the sounds you hear.

THINKING ABOUT... *Composing and improvising*

Writing music is called composing, while making up music as you go along is called improvising ... but, in fact, these are very similar activities. Sing a few random notes, or play them on an instrument. You've just improvised a tune! Can you play the same tune again? If you record it in some way, or even write it down, then you've just composed a piece of music. Lots of composers start writing by improvising tunes.

In Japan, taiko drumming groups like *Kodo* (est. 1981) play a mixture of fixed and improvised rhythms. Because of their thunderous sounds, taiko drums are often used in film soundtracks.

In most pieces composed for orchestra, every note that each
musician plays has been written down in the score, a set of fixed
parts that the players follow. The piece can sound different in each
performance, but the actual notes will always be the same. However,
a jazz tune like 'Round Midnight by *Thelonious Monk* (1917–1982)
is played quite differently every time. We can still recognize the
chords and the melody, but recordings—by *Chet Baker* (1929–1988)
on trumpet, *Wes Montgomery* (1923–1968) on guitar or *Mary Lou
Williams* (1910–1981) on piano—are all interpretations of the piece.
In jazz it's quite normal to begin by playing the original tune and
then improvise around it, with different musicians taking turns to
make up their own solo. This gives jazz concerts a special energy
and excitement, as no two performances are the same.

Many very good musicians say they can't compose music. But why
not give it a go—you might find it easier than you expect. If your tune
sounds a bit like something else, try changing it slightly or adding a
surprising element—eventually you'll make something unique!

Percussion

How do you feel when you hear the sound of drums?

Beats and grooves created by percussion instruments can immediately make us want to dance or march in time with their rhythm. Percussion instruments can be "unpitched," meaning they don't have a particular note, or "pitched," where they have one or several notes. A xylophone, with its individual wooden keys, is a pitched percussion instrument, as is a West African talking drum. This drum is designed to change pitch when its leather or rope strings, called tension cords, are squeezed by the performer.

The beat or pulse is the unit of time that music is divided into. Musicians count beats to keep in time with one another while they are playing, and dancers move their bodies to the beat. When you listen to a piece of music, see if you can work out how many beats there are, and which beats are strong and which are weak. In most pop music, you will hear four beats: 1-2-3-4, 1-2-3-4. In reggae, the groove is quite different: beat 2 and beat 4—the offbeats—take the lead: 1-2-3-4. A waltz always has three beats in a bar: 1-2-3, 1-2-3. There are other ways of dividing up the beats, too. Many musical styles, including samba, use polyrhythms—this is where two or more rhythms are played at the same time. For instance, one musician might play in fours, another in threes.

FARRUQ IBN ABD AL-LATIF *Drawing of Al-Jazari's music machine, a wooden boat filled with automaton musicians*, 1315

We've invented interesting ways of creating rhythms, too. In the 13th century, Turkish engineer **Ismail Al-Jazari** (1136–1206) created a kind of drum machine operated by pegs and levers. Hundreds of years before computers were invented, it could be programmed to play different beats.

The drum kit, invented in 1909, allowed drummers to play many different rhythms at once. **Viola Smith** (1912–2020), who played in the swing style, had a kit that included two high-mounted tom-toms; **Tony Allen** (1940–2020), who invented a style called afrobeat, played so many grooves at the same time he had to be replaced by four drummers when he left his band; while rock drummer **Dave Grohl** (b. 1969) learned to play on pillows to get his distinctive bold beats.

JOHANNES VERMEER *A Young Woman Standing at a Virginal,*
c. 1670–1672

THINKING ABOUT... *The piano*

In this picture by Dutch artist *Johannes Vermeer* (1632–1675), a
young woman stands at an early keyboard called a virginal—a small
harpsichord. Music-making was fashionable in the houses of wealthy
European families, and expensive instruments like this one were
played on their own, or used to accompany another singer or player.
J. S. Bach (1685–1750) wrote *The Well Tempered Clavier*, a set of pieces
that helped players learn the 12 major and 12 minor keys.

Around 1700, *Bartolomeo Cristofori* (1655–1731) invented the
fortepiano (meaning in Italian "loud-quiet"), an early version of the
modern piano. While the earlier harpsichord plucked metal strings,
with every note the same volume, the piano used a system of
hammers to hit the strings. Players could control the loudness of each
note depending on how hard they hit the key. That's why the piano is
considered both a percussion instrument and a stringed instrument!
Virtuoso players like *Clara Schumann* (1819–1896) showed off the
piano's amazing sound. She performed with the best orchestras
across Europe, and composed music, too.

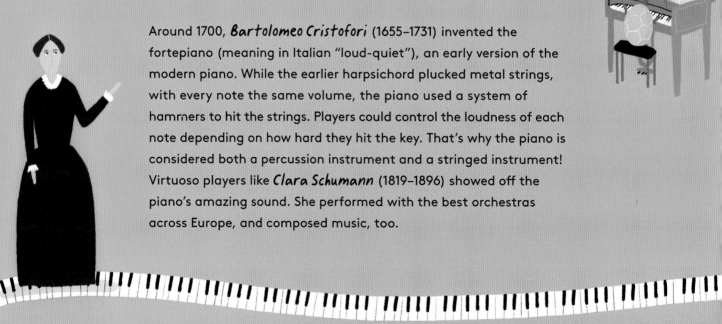

As pianos became much more common, different styles of piano music started to appear. In a street known as Tin Pan Alley in New York, teams of musicians wrote songs for people to play at home. In 1899, *Maple Leaf Rag*, written by *Scott Joplin* (1868–1917), kickstarted a craze for ragtime music. Its off-beat rhythms would influence the sound of jazz in the 20th century.

From the intertwined melodies of Bach's pieces for keyboard, to the energetic jazz piano of *Art Tatum* (1909–1956), from the playful Cuban grooves of *Rubén González* (1919–2003) to the soulful classical R&B of *Alicia Keys* (b. 1981), the piano has played an important part in defining many types of music.

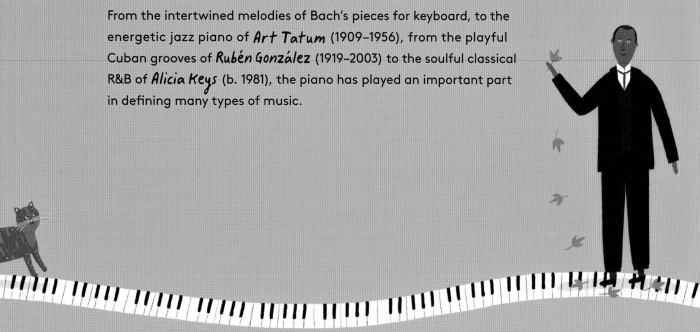

Wind

Find an empty bottle and blow across (not into!) the hole at the top. At first you might just hear a noise like wind blowing, but with practice you'll be able to produce a note with a clear pitch. Now partly fill the bottle with water and blow again... does the note have a higher pitch? By changing the amount of air inside the bottle, you've changed the note. This is how all wind instruments work, whether using finger holes, keys, slides or valves.

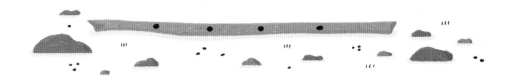

Wind instruments were some of the first musical tools humans invented. In 2008, archaeologists discovered the remains of a c. 40,000-year-old flute made from hollowed-out bone in a cave in Hohle Fels, Germany. It has finger holes, carefully spaced to produce different pitches, just like recorders do today.

Even the slightest change in the shape of a wind instrument can alter the sound it makes. Jazz trumpeter *Dizzy Gillespie* (1917–1993) played in a fast, frenetic style called bebop. His uniquely shaped trumpet came about quite by accident! When it fell over on stage, its bell bent upward. He had it fixed, but realized he preferred the tone of the bent instrument, so he had a new one designed specially for him.

The painting below shows a musician playing an early version of the bagpipes. The canvas sack, which he squeezes as he plays, acts as an extra pair of lungs to pump air through its wooden pipes. The *yidaki*, or didgeridoo, has been played by Aboriginal people in the Northern Territory of Australia for thousands of years. Players like *Djalu Gurruwiwi* (b. c. 1940) use a technique called circular breathing which produces a continuous note with no break. All wind players need a lot of puff!

PIETER BRUEGEL THE ELDER *The Peasant Dance*, c. 1569

THINKING ABOUT... *The Orchestra*

Have you ever played in an orchestra? Orchestras as we know them today started out in the 17th century and still sit in more or less the same arrangement. British composer *Benjamin Britten* (1913–1976) wrote *The Young Person's Guide to the Orchestra* to introduce listeners to each group of instruments in turn. Orchestra players are arranged in a semi-circle so they can all see the conductor, who stands in the middle waving a baton to help everyone play at the right time. The conductor works with the players to decide how the music should sound, and sets the speed, or tempo, for each piece.

Orchestras vary in size from under 50 players—a chamber orchestra —to over 100 players—a symphony orchestra. But symphonies by Austrian composer *Gustav Mahler* (1860–1911) were written for 120 musicians, creating a huge sound! Most large cities have at least one orchestra and a concert hall where they perform their repertoire of music, including symphonies and concertos—pieces written for a solo player, accompanied by an orchestra.

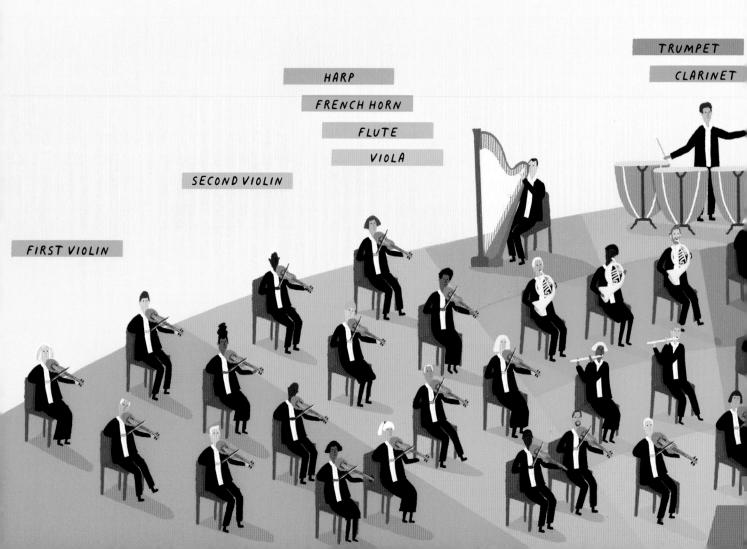

TRUMPET

CLARINET

HARP

FRENCH HORN

FLUTE

VIOLA

SECOND VIOLIN

FIRST VIOLIN

The Recycled Orchestra, founded in Paraguay in 2006, plays on instruments made from scrap metal like oil drums, cans, forks, keys and bottle tops salvaged from a landfill site.

The West-Eastern Divan Orchestra, founded by musician *Daniel Barenboim* (b. 1942) and writer *Edward Said* (1935–2003), unites musicians from countries across the Middle East, including Egypt, Iran, Israel and Palestine. By playing together, the musicians are sending the world an important message about peace and unity. The Chineke! Orchestra, founded in the UK by bassist *Chi-chi Nwanoku* (b. 1956), is mostly made up of Black, Asian and ethnically diverse musicians. They perform a wide range of music, including works by under-represented writers such as the Black British composer *Samuel Coleridge-Taylor* (1875-1912).

PERCUSSION

TROMBONE

BASSOON

TUBA

OBOE

DOUBLE BASS

CELLO

CONDUCTOR

Strings

Stringed instruments come in many sizes, but they all work in the same way. When a string vibrates, the sound it makes depends on three things—the string's thickness, its length and how tight it is stretched. You can test this yourself by stretching a rubber band. Twang it and you'll hear a note. Pull tighter and you'll hear a higher pitched note. But don't stretch it too far or it'll snap! At the 1969 Woodstock music festival in the U.S., *Jimi Hendrix* (1942–1970) broke one of the strings on his electric guitar. But people didn't notice—he just carried on playing.

These days, most strings are metal or plastic, but in the past they were made from sheep's intestines. To make the strings vibrate, they can be plucked like on a guitar or an oud, hammered like a cimbalom, or played with a bow like a violin. Plucked or hammered strings make a sound with a loud start, which quickly fades away, while a bowed string produces notes that last much longer. In classical Indian music, a large stringed instrument called the tanpura is used to create a constant note called a drone throughout a piece. A melody is played or sung over the top.

OUD   DULCIMER   TANPURA

When strings are attached to a hollow "box," the sound of their vibrations is amplified, or made louder; the larger the instrument, the deeper the pitch. Famous string players often play very old, valuable instruments, finely carved from wood. British cellist *Sheku Kanneh-Mason* (b. 1999) plays an Amati cello made in 1610 that has a rich tone, and Scottish violinist *Nicola Benedetti* (b. 1987) plays a 1717 Stradivarius violin that has a high, sweet sound. Both instruments were made by experts from the same small town of Cremona in Italy where crafting instruments was their profession.

Electronics

For thousands of years, people made music using only acoustic instruments that need to be struck, bowed or blown. But in the 20th and 21st centuries, we started using electronics to make music.

In 1896, inventor *Thaddeus Cahill* (1867–1934) developed the first electronic instrument, the Telharmonium. It was an enormous electronic organ, weighing 200 tons (the weight of 10 buses) and costing $6 million today! Only three were ever made and, sadly, none survive. We don't even have a recording of what the Telharmonium sounded like. Perhaps it's not surprising that it wasn't successful!

Film still from *The Day the Earth Stood Still*, 1951

WE ARE THE ROBOTS!

The theremin, invented in 1920 by Russian engineer *Leon Theremin* (1896–1993), created a spooky sound unlike anything people had heard before. Musician *Clara Rockmore* (1911–1988) was involved in its design and played it in front of huge audiences across America. You changed the sound by moving your hands in front of two antennae —one controlled the pitch, the other the volume. Because it sounded so strange, the theremin was used in films about aliens, such as *Bernard Hermann's* (1911–1975) soundtrack for the film *The Day the Earth Stood Still*.

As time went on, more new inventions transformed music. Electric guitars helped create the brash sound of pop music in the 1950s. In the 1960s American engineer *Robert Moog* (1934–2005) developed the synthesizer, which could produce thousands of different sounds. The German group *Kraftwerk* (est. 1970) dressed up as robots and performed music that was almost entirely electronic, as if made by machines. Synths would change the sound of music forever! In the 1980s electronic drum machines like the Roland TR-808 helped to create the rhythms of hip hop and house music.

The influence of electronics continues today, and now much of the music we listen to is created using computers.

Music and our brains

Sounds and tunes fire up our brains! Neurons—the tiny cells that carry messages from one part of the body to another—respond to music by releasing chemicals that make us feel joyful or relaxed. We can even get the chills or goosebumps. We don't just use our ears to enjoy music. Vibrations, which we feel through our sense of touch, stimulate our brains too. Scottish percussionist *Evelyn Glennie* (b. 1965)—who had lost her hearing by the age of 12—uses her whole body to feel the music she's playing; she performs barefoot so that she can sense the music's vibrations and beats.

Film still from *The Wizard of Oz*, 1939

Though we all prefer different combinations of rhythms, notes and chords, there are certain melodies that many people respond to in the same way. Different intervals—the distance between two notes—can affect the way we feel when we're listening. *Over The Rainbow*, sung by *Judy Garland* (1922–1969) in the film *The Wizard of Oz*, includes an octave interval ("Somewhere...") followed by an interval called a sixth ("Bluebirds fly..."). Giant leaps from one note to another, combined with the lyrics, help us understand Dorothy's longing for a better world. Have a think about a song you like. How do things like the tune, words, or the rhythm affect you?

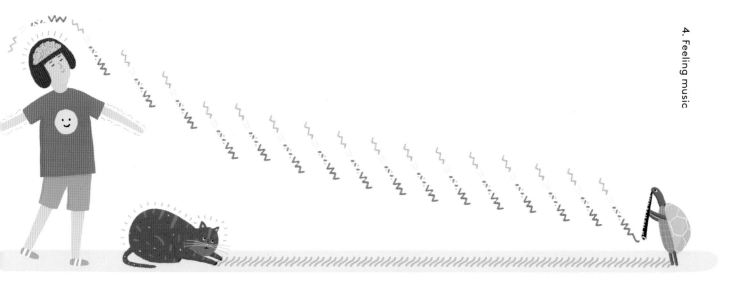

When we play a piece of music, we learn the notes by practising the same bits over and over again. This way, we lock them into the part of our brain where long-term memories are stored. Once you've learned to play it without thinking too hard, performing your favorite tune is as easy as counting to ten. So don't give up!

Music brings us together

Music can encourage feelings of belonging—to a country, a club or a group. In Rio de Janeiro, Brazil, at the annual Carnival, musicians and dancers from hundreds of samba schools across the country dress in colorful costumes and parade through the city. Samba schools are not actually places that teach samba, but music and dance clubs that were first set up in the 1920s to bring people from the same neighborhood together. Centuries before, the rhythms of samba had been brought to Brazil by enslaved people from West Africa.

Sharing music encourages us to feel that we have something in common. The sight and sound of sports stars singing along to the national anthem at events like the Olympic Games often inspires a feeling of pride in our country. Next time you watch a sporting ceremony, compare the tunes. Listen out for marches with trumpet fanfares and drum rolls, and slower hymns with soaring strings.

DR MARTIN LUTHER KING, JR. at the Civil Rights Movement's March
on Washington, August 28, 1963

As well as bringing us together, music can inspire great change.
It was an important part of the U.S. Civil Rights movement in the
1960s that demanded equal rights for African Americans. Singers
Mahalia Jackson (1911–1972), *Bob Dylan* (b. 1941) and *Joan Baez*
(b. 1941), among others, sang to a crowd of 250,000 people at the
March on Washington in 1963, where *Dr Martin Luther King Jr.*
(1929–1968) delivered his famous speech, *I Have a Dream*. Songs like
We Shall Overcome and *The Times They Are A-Changin'* didn't just
use inspirational lyrics—their rousing tunes helped people understand
that the world could be transformed into a better place. Perhaps
one day you will write a song that helps create change?

Music tells stories

Have you ever put a shell to your ear and heard the sound of the sea? Or held a rainstick—an instrument from Chile that's made from a hollowed cactus filled with pebbles—and tipped it to hear a sound like cascading rain? Many musicians have written pieces based on sounds from nature. The French composer *Claude Debussy* (1862–1918) was inspired by the sea when he wrote *La Mer* in 1905, conjuring the sound of rippling waves and water droplets with the instruments of the orchestra. He kept a framed print of *The Great Wave* by Japanese artist *Katsushika Hokusai* (1760–1849) on the wall of his studio in Paris.

Some composers think of instruments as different characters, like actors in a play. In *Peter and the Wolf*, a piece of music written for a narrator and an orchestra by Russian composer *Sergei Prokofiev* (1891–1953), the instruments help to tell the story. Prokofiev chose a flute for the bird, whose high-pitched trills sing a chirpy tune. Peter is played by strings, his grandfather by a bassoon, the wolf by a horn, the duck by an oboe, the cat by a clarinet and hunters by the drums.

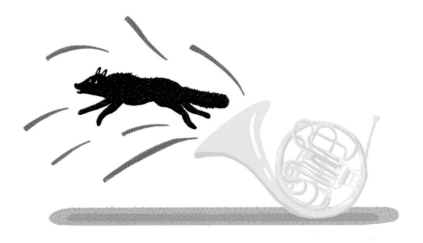

KATSUSHIKA HOKUSAI, *The Great Wave*, c. 1831

In 1899 Debussy was amazed by an Indonesian gamelan performance he saw in Paris. The gamelan, which means "to hammer" in Javanese, is a kind of orchestra filled with bronze metallophones, gongs, drums and sometimes strings and flutes. It's used in theater and shadow puppet plays that tell folk stories from Bali and Java in Indonesia. One famous tale is that of Lokanata, the first gamelan orchestra, whose three gongs were used to summon the gods.

THINKING ABOUT... Music for film

In the late 1880s, audiences were amazed when they saw moving images on screen for the first time. By 1920, there were more than 20,000 movie theaters in the U.S., and studios in Hollywood were making 800 films a year. In these silent movies, there was no sound —just images. But filmmakers soon realized that music could help the audience understand the story and connect with the characters. So in movie theaters, music would be played live by a pianist or organist, who would often improvise while the film was showing. Comedies starring *Charlie Chaplin* (1889–1977) became associated with frantic piano playing, which created tension, humor and excitement. To help with musical storytelling, the Mighty Wurlitzer organ was invented to imitate hundreds of instruments; it also provided sound effects like horses' hooves.

The Jazz Singer (1927) was the first film to have a soundtrack featuring speech, sound effects, songs and music. It was a huge hit. Within a couple of years, pianos and organs began to disappear from movie theaters as all films came with a unique soundtrack. Ever since then, the music accompanying a film—called the score—has become a crucial part of the entertainment. India now has the largest film industry in the world, with around 2,000 films being produced every year. Music is especially important, with actors often breaking into song and dance routines.

While most of us notice a theme song in a film, the effect of background music is less obvious. But, take the score away from a car chase, a romantic moment or a dream sequence, and you'll find that the magic is gone! Next time you're watching your favorite movie, listen carefully to the music... How is it making you feel?

Sometimes scores are so recognisable and popular, they become as famous as the film itself. Soundtracks by composers like *Ennio Morricone* (1928–2020), who wrote scores for the Spaghetti Westerns of the 1960s, or *John Williams* (b. 1932), who has composed music for *Jaws*, *Star Wars* and *Harry Potter*, are played in concert halls around the world.

5

SEEING MUSIC
How is music written down and passed on?

I'm Anoushka Shankar, and I started learning the sitar from my father Ravi when I was seven. Some of the music I play is over 3,000 years old.

The oral tradition

Throughout history, humans have found many ways to write music down. But lots of music isn't written on a page at all. Since ancient times, songs, rhythms and ways of playing instruments have been passed on from one musician to another by what we call the oral tradition—oral means "spoken." A grandparent singing a folk song or nursery rhyme to a child may have learnt it from their own grandparents 80 years earlier. But music changes every time it is played. The tune the child hears may be very similar to the one their ancestors sung, but it is unlikely to be exactly the same... Each new performer may add their own ideas to the music, or may misremember the old melody.

Before the invention of paper, printing or sound recordings, the oral tradition was the main way of passing on music. No one knows who first wrote certain songs or tunes, but the music has lived on for hundreds, even thousands of years. From the stories sung by the griots of Mali or Senegal (see page 26) to the sacred songs of the Navajo or Cherokee nations, music has been kept alive through ceremonies, festivals and celebrations. Versions of ancient chants and prayers, composed in India as long ago as 1500 BCE, are still played today by musicians like *Anoushkar Shankar* (b. 1981). It's not just tunes and songs that are passed on from generation to generation, but also styles of playing—learning a musical instrument involves watching, listening to and copying the teacher.

Music on the page

Because music is something we HEAR, turning it into something we SEE is rather tricky. Some of the earliest examples of written music are the Hurrian Songs, which were engraved on clay tablets in c. 1400 BCE, in an area now known as Syria. We don't know exactly how to read the music but we can read their writing, which includes instructions for tuning a lyre. Many ways of writing music down use lines or symbols called neumes, showing whether the tune should go up or down—as on these scrolls created by Buddhist monks.

Three leaves from a musical score used in rituals by Buddhist monks with the notation for voice, drums, trumpets, horns and cymbals.

Around 1000 CE, an Italian Monk called *Guido d'Arezzo* (c. 995–1050) drew individual music notes on a stave made of horizontal lines. By the 18th century, this method of notating music had been developed further and was used all over Europe, allowing bigger groups of musicians to play more complicated music together.

The score (the music written on the page) could tell everyone in the orchestra which notes to play and what rhythm to play them in, and also how loud or soft they should be. Because musical scores are so detailed, we are able to accurately play music long after the composer has died. If Norwegian composer *Edvard Grieg* (1843–1907) walked into a concert hall today, he would hear *In the Hall of the Mountain King* played exactly as he'd written it.

Sometimes, the discovery of long-forgotten scores brings new pieces to our attention. In 1933, *Florence Price* (1887–1953) was the first African American female composer to have her work played by an orchestra in a US concert hall. Years later, it was thought that most of her music had been lost. But, in 2009, a set of scores was found in an abandoned house in Illinois—now, her music can be performed again, and enjoyed by future generations.

THINKING ABOUT...*Reading music*

If you're learning an instrument, you may be used to seeing music that looks like this—a set of notes that at first seem to dance around on the lines in quite random ways. But once you know how to read them, you'll be able to play almost any tune without having to hear it first. Here are a few things to look out for:

The *stave* is the five parallel lines that notes sit on. A *clef* tells you the pitch of the *notes*. The clefs you'll see most often are the *treble clef* for higher-pitched instruments like the flute, and the *bass clef* for lower-pitched instruments such as the double bass. Piano music uses both clefs—treble for the right hand, bass for the left.

It can be helpful to think of the stave as a ladder. As the notes climb it, the pitch gets higher. To remember the sequence of notes, you can learn some simple phrases:

TREBLE CLEF

E G B D F   F A C E

Every Green Bus Drives Fast   F-A-C-E

STAVE

BASS CLEF

G B D F A   A C E G

Grizzly Bears Don't Fear Anything   All Cows Eat Grass

You can also make up your own rhymes or codes—anything goes, as long as you can remember it!

Now we've looked at pitch, let's take a look at how we can read the rhythm. The notes all have different values:

A *semibreve* lasts 4 beats.

A *minim* lasts 2 beats.

A *crotchet* lasts 1 beat.

A *quaver* is a half beat.

Can you spot them in this piece of music? You can also look out for some other instructions that are written here, too:

TIME SIGNATURE

KEY SIGNATURE

BAR LINE   DYNAMIC   ARTICULATION

Time Signature—Here, a time signature of 4/4 tells you that there are four crotchet beats in every bar.

Key Signature—This tells you whether there are any sharps (♯) or flats (♭) in the piece. These are the black notes on a piano keyboard. This piece is in the key of D major, so there are two sharps, F and C.

Bar lines—Music is divided into bars, separated by bar lines. At the end of the piece is a double bar line.

Dynamics—Instructions for how to play the piece are often written in Italian. *f* stands for *forte*, which means "loud." *p* stands for *piano*, which means "quiet."

Articulation—A dot above the note means play it *staccato* (short and spiky); a slur above a group of notes means to play it smoothly.

Draw five lines, and see if you can make up your own piece of music!

WASSILY KANDINSKY, *Composition No. 8*, 1923

Drawing music

In the paintings of **Wassily Kandinsky** (1866–1944), a wild mix of colorful shapes, straight and curved lines criss-cross in different directions. Kandinsky, who also played the cello, had synaesthesia—which causes the five senses (sight, sound, touch, smell and taste) to swap around or mix together. This meant he "saw" sounds, "heard" colors and shapes, and often gave his pictures musical titles. He told of an evening, at the opera, where a vision of a painting appeared before his eyes as he was listening to the music.

Many artists, writers and musicians have described mixing music and pictures in this way. As a boy, composer and saxophonist **Anthony Braxton** (b. 1945) was inspired to "draw" the saxophone solos he heard. In his compositions, instead of writing down particular notes, he creates pictures that express how he wants the music to sound.

Describing a piece of music in pictures is personal, and we'll all do it differently. But we can agree on some things music and art share. There's composition—the way everything is arranged on the page or in a piece. There's rhythm—repeated beats, or repeated patterns of lines and shapes. And there's harmony—the way sounds, textures, colors or shapes blend together. Look up a painting by *Piet Mondrian* (1872–1944), *Broadway Boogie Woogie*, which is named after a street in New York full of music theaters, Broadway, and a popular musical style of the time, Boogie Woogie. Look at the colorful grid of squares and lines. Does it make you imagine beats and rhythms? Another artist, *Josef Albers* (1888–1976), designed covers for jazz records using combinations of dots and squares. Next time you listen to a piece of music, try drawing it too!

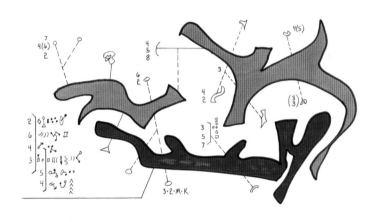

NO. 363 h

ANTHONY BRAXTON, *Falling River Music (363h)*, 2004–present

PERFORMING AND LISTENING TO MUSIC

Where and how can we listen to music?

I'm David Bowie and I was born in the UK in 1947. I created the character Ziggy Stardust and dressed up in space-age costumes for my live shows and videos.

Big spaces

Listening to music as part of a big crowd is an unforgettable experience. At the Colosseum in Rome, home to chariot races and gladiator fights, the ancient Romans played music to crowds of 80,000 people! In the Middle Ages, music was performed in cathedrals like Notre Dame in Paris, which echoed the sound around its tall ceilings and stone walls. *Giovanni Gabrieli* (c. 1554–1612) wrote music to be played in St Mark's Basilica in Venice. He placed groups of musicians playing different tunes all around the church, creating an early version of surround sound. From the 18th century onwards, concert halls were specially built for music performances. Architects carefully chose the shapes of buildings to improve the acoustics— the way music sounds in a room.

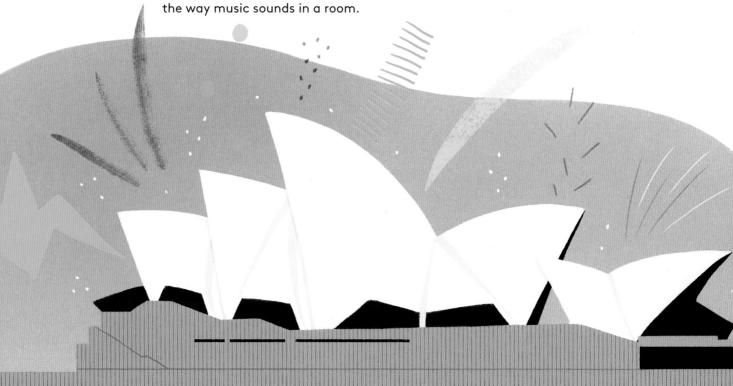

With the invention of electric instruments, amplifiers and speakers in the 20th century, it became possible to have music concerts on a different scale from anything seen before. While The Beatles were the first band to do a stadium tour in 1965, recent stars like *Beyoncé* (b. 1981) and the K-pop band *BTS* (est. 2010) play to far more people across the world. *Ed Sheeran*'s (b. 1991) recent ÷ *(Divide)* tour lasted almost three years and had a total audience of nearly 9 million people!

In 1969, the Woodstock festival in the U.S. started a craze for huge gatherings of music fans. Every year, thousands camp in a small village in Somerset, UK, at the Glastonbury Festival. With hundreds of bands playing over a weekend, festivals like Mawazine in Rabat, Morocco, are great places to discover new music. In 2020, thousands of performers streamed concerts directly into the homes of their fans via the internet during the COVID-19 pandemic.

Spectacular performers

Musical performances are made even more dramatic by dancers, costumes, lighting and other special effects. Audiences have been entertained for hundreds of years by kabuki theatre in Japan, where performers in bold outfits flew through the air, attached to invisible wires. The Ballet Russes, that performed in Europe from 1909–1929, worked with famous artists whose designs brought ballets like *Igor Stravinsky*'s (1882–1971) *The Firebird* to life. Today, musicals on Broadway in New York and in London's West End compete to dazzle, from the sparkling Cave of Wonders in *Aladdin* to a real helicopter landing on stage in *Miss Saigon*!

UTAGAWA KUNISADA, Portrait of the famous kabuki actor Kawarasaki Gonjuro I in the play *The Battles of Coxinga*, 1861

Pop and rock musicians also dress up to perform for the crowd. In his *Spiders From Mars* tour, **David Bowie** (1947–2016) took to the stage dressed as Ziggy Stardust, a space-age alien rockstar in an orange wig, sparkly jumpsuit and high platform shoes. One of the first bands to create an amazing spectacle at their rock concerts was **Pink Floyd** (est. 1965). For their tour of *The Wall* (1980–1981), they used lights, film projections, enormous puppets, and even had an a 36-foot-high wall built live on stage each night, which was then destroyed at the end of the concert.

In 1981, MTV (Music Television) was launched and bands created stylish videos to make their songs stand out. These days, YouTube allows videos to be shared by millions of people. Pop group **OK Go** (est. 1998) are known for producing incredible videos, like *The One Moment* and *I Won't Let You Down*.

THINKING ABOUT... *How music is recorded*

A machine called the phonograph, which means "sound writing," was invented in 1877 by **Thomas Edison** (1847–1931). It used a needle to record sound vibrations onto cylinders covered with tin foil (and later with wax). The sound could be played back, though not in great quality—and he abandoned his invention to work on the light bulb! The gramophone, invented in 1887 by **Emile Berliner** (1851–1929), recorded sound onto flat, spinning discs called records. These early machines were large and clunky to carry around, but they worked. Composer **Béla Bartók** (1881–1945) used a phonograph to record folk melodies sung by the Magyar people in Hungary and Romania, and worked these tunes into his own compositions. Their performances have been kept for all time!

Explorer **Captain Scott** (1868–1912) took a gramophone on his Antarctic expedition in 1910, along with a selection of records to listen to on cold, dark nights. Scott and his crew never returned from their mission. But their gramophone, found buried in ice in the abandoned camp, still worked – and is now kept in a museum.

As records and radio broadcasts became popular to listen to at home, more musicians went to recording studios to cut discs of their music. Better microphones, used to record singers like *Billie Holiday* (1915–1959), could capture performances in much more detail, which changed the way people made music. While earlier singers had to have really loud voices to be heard over the band, the microphone led to a new, quieter style of singing called crooning by stars like *Nat King Cole* (1919–1965), *Frank Sinatra* (1915–1998) and, later, the whispering *Joao Gilberto* (1931–2019).

Other techniques like mixing in stereo (where different sounds come out of each speaker) and multi-track tape recording (layering many sounds on top of one another) meant that in the studio, producers could create songs that sounded quite different to live shows. In the 1960s, *The Beach Boys* (est. 1961) spent months recording lush layers of vocal harmonies. While in the 20th century most bands had to travel to big studios like the famous Abbey Road in London, today home computers contain everything we need to record music.

Music at home

Until gramophones, the only tunes you could listen to at home were those you played yourself—on your own or with friends. Chamber music written for small groups of instruments was fashionable in Europe from the 18th century, when it became easier to print and share music. Two hundred years later, people were still buying sheet music to play parlor songs on pianos in their own homes, like *I Love You Truly* by **Carrie Jacobs-Bond** (1862–1946), which sold over a million copies.

Records soon overtook the fever for printed music! In the USA, 140 million records were sold in 1921. But other new entertainment systems were not far behind. In the 1920s, radio stations all over the world started broadcasting, sending the same programs out to thousands of people at the same time. As more and more people were able to buy wireless radios for their homes, families would tune in to listen to news, entertainment programs—and, of course, music.

As the quality of music systems improved, people started to spend more money on getting the best hi-fi speakers, amplifiers and record players. In 1979 the Walkman changed the way we listen to music forever, as it was possible to listen to music cassettes while going for a walk, traveling to work or even sunbathing! In the 1990s, CDs (compact discs) took over from records and cassettes as the main way of listening to music at home.

In 2001, Apple released the first iPod and, since then, much of the music we listen to is downloaded digitally or streamed from the Internet. These days it's not unusual to find every member of a family listening to a different piece of music at the same time on their own device—the days of families huddled around a piano or a radio are over!

7

WHAT'S NEXT FOR MUSIC?

I'm AIVA and I'm a composer, but I'm not a human being, I'm a computer algorithm!

Rise of the machines

From the piano to the Internet, new technology has transformed the way we play, write and listen to music. In 1997, *Jyoti Mishra* (b. 1966) had a global hit with the song *Your Woman*, which he released under the name "White Town." It was the first chart-topper to be bedroom produced—created by one person at home, using a cheap computer and an old tape machine. Since then, the quality of music made on computers has improved so much that many successful albums have been created on laptops rather than in recording studios. *Billie Eilish* (b. 2001), working with her brother *Finneas* (b. 1997), recorded her first album *When We All Fall Asleep, Where Do We Go?* in her bedroom in 2019. The album has now been streamed billions of times!

New instruments and music-making tools are being invented all the time. Some are based on familiar instruments. The Roli Seaboard is shaped like a piano keyboard, but its rubber keys have touch sensors that control the sound in different ways. Other musical inventions generate loops of sounds that can be rearranged. The Ableton Live program is used by musicians like **Daft Punk** (est. 1993), who create tracks and remix them when they perform.

Many apps and games that allow people to make music at home use visual graphics to inspire creativity. On *Isle of Tune*, players compose a piece by designing an island world complete with roads, houses, street lamps, plants and trees (the "instruments"). As cars (the "players") drive around the island, different sounds are triggered. Players can share their compositions and like the creations of others.

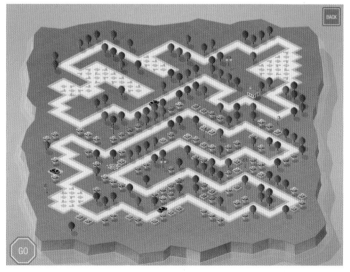

ISLE OF TUNE An island based on the theme song for the Disney Pixar movie *Up!*, 2018

Interactive music

Have you ever noticed the music soundtrack of a computer game changing as you play? There may be a restful tune for a scene on a calm beach but as you approach a dark cave, a spooky track starts playing... Composers like *Yoko Shimomura* (b. 1967) create different pieces for each part of the game, and the music gradually adapts as the characters move around the world.

We call this kind of music interactive—which means that our actions affect the sounds we hear. Smart watches and phones can detect changes in your body, such as your heart rate or blood pressure. The app Weav responds by changing the speed and intensity of the music you're listening to depending on how you're moving. If you're running fast, it sets the music to a faster tempo to match your speed.

More than ever, music is being made and listened to on computers. But it's still made by humans... isn't it? **AIVA** (created in 2016) is an AI or Artificial Intelligence composer. This powerful computer program analyzes millions of pieces of music—then creates its own! AIVA writes in many different musical styles and has released two albums. Future AI composers will be able to predict what kind of music we like but also how we will respond to it. How do you feel about a computer being programmed to write a piece of music intentionally to make you cry?

Even though so much has changed in our world, music will always be important to us. We still play flutes and bang on drums, just as our ancestors were doing thousands of years ago. In 50 years' time, do you think we will still be playing pianos and guitars, or will we also be playing instruments that respond to our movements in a totally different way? Only time will tell!

TIMELINE OF INVENTIONS

BCE stands for 'Before the Common Era'
CE stands for 'Common Era'

Historians originally thought that Jesus was born in the year zero, at the start of the Common Era. Events that occurred before his birth are counted back from the year zero, and events after his birth are counted forwards. When it is obvious a date is in the Common Era, the letters CE are not used.

FROM AROUND 40,000 YEARS AGO

Early musicians make drums, shakers and other instruments from wood, stretched animal skins, seedpods, stones and shells. They also carve flutes from pieces of bone or ivory.

AROUND 2500 BCE

In Mesopotamia, "gut" strings made from the tightly stretched intestines of sheep and cows are used to make lyres and harps. Music is written on clay tablets in a language called cuneiform.

AROUND 1500 BCE

Instrument makers across the world –from Egypt to Scandinavia– craft pieces of metal into horns and trumpets. Their loud, bright sounds can travel long distances.

AROUND 1020 CE

The musical stave is invented by the Italian monk Guido d'Arezzo. With this way of writing music down, tunes can be read straight from the page, like a piece of text. Monks spend many months copying music out by hand.

AROUND 1235

In West Africa in the courts of the Mali Empire, musicians called griots (or jelis) play a central role. The djembe drum, invented by the Mandinke people, grows in popularity.

AROUND 1500

New inventions in ship building, sails and navigation tools allow ships to travel vast distances. Tragically, over the next 300 years, 12 million Africans are transported and forced to work on plantations in the Americas and the Caribbean. They take their music with them—and many new musical styles are born.

AROUND 1300 BCE

In China, sets of large decorated bells cast in bronze are played in court ceremonies. Each is tuned to a different note. Musicians perform on an instrument called the qin (whose strings are made of silk) and a set of bamboo pipes called a sheng.

AROUND 200 BCE

The hydraulis water organ, the first known keyboard instrument, is invented in Greece. It is made popular by the Romans, who use it in theater and gladiator shows.

AROUND 800 CE

The four-stringed oud is introduced to Europe by North Africans who settle in the south of Spain. This will lead to the creation of the Spanish lute and, in the 1500s, the guitar.

FROM 1530

In Italy, studios of instrument makers like the Amati and Stradivari families craft thousands of violins and cellos—many of which are still played today. Since the invention of the printing press in 1440, music can be copied quickly and distributed widely.

FROM AROUND 1700

The modern sitar emerges in India during the Mughal Empire. It has its roots in both the ancient veena and the Persian setar, and defines the sound of North Indian classical music.

AROUND 1700

The fortepiano is invented by Bartolomeo Cristofori in Italy. Unlike the earlier harpsichord, its strings are struck by a set of hammers inside the instrument, allowing it to be played loudly or quietly. The piano will become one of the world's most popular instruments.

1877

Thomas Edison invents a machine called the phonograph, which can record and play back music. Flat discs called records will be a popular way of listening to music for the next 100 years.

1877–1925

Microphones allow musical performances to be recorded in more and more detail. Even quiet or whispering singing styles can be heard over the noise of a band.

1920s

Radio brings live and recorded music into people's homes. Thousands of people are able to listen to the same performers at the same time.

1963–1964

Robert Moog invents the synthesizer. With it, musicians can experiment and create thousands of unique sounds—all from a single keyboard.

1979

A portable cassette player called the Sony Walkman is designed in Japan. It allows people to listen to music as they travel around—on a pair of headphones plugged in to the machine.

1980s

The Fairlight CMI, created in Australia, was one of the world's first samplers. A sample is a small slice of recorded music or sound that can be played back at different pitches or speeds. Later samplers were important in hip hop and dance music.

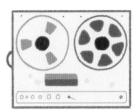

EARLY 1930s

In America, the first electric guitars, which will become the sound of pop music in the 1950s and '60s, are created.

1940s

Jukeboxes, first invented in the 1890s, become popular in bars and coffee shops across America. They are coin operated and play jazz, swing and rock'n'roll records.

1955

The multitrack tape recorder is used by musicians Les Paul and Mary Ford. They create recordings that combine many sounds and harmonies.

1982

Compact discs, which store music tracks digitally, are launched. They soon replace records and cassettes as the most popular way to listen to music.

1989

The Internet is invented by Tim Berners-Lee. Pieces of music can be sent across the world as digital files. Ten years later, portable MP3 players like iPods allow people to listen to vast libraries of music on the go.

2006

Music is streamed on platforms like Spotify. Listeners can choose from millions of tracks by thousands of performers, for free.

GLOSSARY

ACOUSTICS the study of the way sound travels in different spaces.

AMPHITHEATER a large, outdoor performance space with seating arranged in steps or tiers.

AMPLIFIER an electronic device attached to an instrument or a microphone. It allows music to be played at a higher volume.

BALLET a dance performed to music, using a particular set of movements and steps, that dates back to the 15th century. Dancers wear special shoes and costumes.

BEBOP a style of jazz that originated in the 1940s, where singers or musicians play fast, complex tunes and rhythms.

BOW a stick for playing a stringed instrument. It's usually tightly strung with horse hair, and creates sound as it passes across the strings.

BRASS INSTRUMENT a wind instrument made of metal such as a trumpet or tuba.

CHAMBER MUSIC music performed by a small group of players.

CHOIR a group of singers. They may sing in unison (where everyone sings the same tune and rhythm) or in harmony (where people sing different notes and parts).

CIRCULAR BREATHING a technique sometimes used by wind players. They breathe in through their nose while blowing air out through their mouth, making a smooth, unbroken sound.

CONCERTO a piece of music usually written for a solo performer accompanied by an orchestra. Concertos became popular in the 18th century.

COMMISSION a piece of music written at the request of another person, who pays the composer for their work.

COMPOSER someone who writes a piece of music or a song.

DAWN CHORUS the singing of birds at the beginning of every new day, usually when the sun rises.

DIDGERIDOO (also *yidaki*) an ancient Australian Aboriginal wind instrument made from a long, hollowed-out tree trunk. Players use circular breathing to make a continuous, deep sound.

DJEMBE a goblet-shaped drum from West Africa, usually made from a single piece of wood. Its skin is tuned by ropes that adjust the tension.

ENSEMBLE a group of musicians playing together.

FANFARE a tune played on brass instruments, usually in a formal ceremony.

FOLK MUSIC the traditional music and songs played and sung by people living in a country or region. Words and melodies are passed down through many generations.

GAMELAN an orchestra of bronze percussion instruments including gongs, chimes and drums. It originated in Bali and Java, in Indonesia.

GOSPEL a style of religious music that emerged in Black Christian churches in the southern states of America in the late 19th century.

GRIOT (also *jeli*) an African musician who is a member of a musical family. In their music and lyrics, they pass on stories of historical events. The tradition can be traced back to the court musicians of the Mali Empire in the 13th century.

HARMONY the blending of musical notes and sounds, usually in a pleasing way.

HIP HOP a style of music that originated in New York in the 1970s. Musicians created new beats and sounds by mixing together clips from existing pieces of music.

HYMN a religious song or prayer set to music.

IMPROVISE to play without following written music.

JAZZ a type of music that emerged in America at the beginning of the 20th century. It shares many features of African folk music: singers and players use off-beat rhythms and polyrhythms, and improvise solos around chords and patterns.

MICROPHONE a device that converts sound waves into an electrical signal, to increase the volume of a singer or performer.

NATIONAL ANTHEM a song or piece of music written to celebrate a country's achievements and its superiority over other nations.

NOTATION a system for writing down music using symbols to represent notes and/or rhythms.

OPERA a musical play with elaborate costumes and solo vocal performances. China and Italy have famous opera traditions.

ORCHESTRA a group of musicians playing together, led by a conductor. Players sit together in groups called sections—strings, brass, woodwind and percussion.

PERCUSSION instruments used for beating a rhythm including drums and shakers. Some percussion instruments also have a pitch, such as xylophones, bells and talking drums.

PHONOGRAPH an early machine for recording and playing music. The first machines recorded on to wax cylinders; later machines called gramophones played records.

PITCH the sound of a note; this can be high or low, depending on the speed of sound waves, or vibrations.

RAGA patterns of notes used in North Indian classical music, which players use to improvise melodies. There are many different ragas, each with their own unique character.

RAP a style of music where lyrics (often rhyming) are spoken over beats.

REGGAE a style of music that originated in the Caribbean in the late 1960s. It uses slow, off-beat rhythms.

RHYTHM a series of beats and sounds, often arranged in a repeating pattern. In a polyrhythm, many overlapping rhythms are played at the same time.

SAMBA a style of music and dance with off-beat rhythms and polyrhythms, that originated in Brazil.

SCORE a handwritten or printed set of musical parts for a piece of music; a film or tv soundtrack is also often called a score.

SITAR a long-necked stringed instrument used in North Indian classical music. Players use a combination of plucked strings and drones, or continuous notes.

SOUNDTRACK music written to accompany a TV show, film, play or computer game.

SOUND WAVES the vibrations in the air that allow sound and music to be heard. Sound waves travel at 343 metres per second.

STAVE a set of five parallel lines on which music notes are written.

STREAMING a way of listening to music, and watching films, over the Internet without downloading it first.

STRINGED INSTRUMENTS musical instruments that have strings; they can be bowed (violin), plucked (sitar) or strummed (guitar)— or a combination of all three.

SYMPHONY a musical piece written for orchestra, usually in four movements, which became popular in the 18th century.

SYNTHESIZER an electronic musical instrument that generates a large range of sounds, usually with a keyboard attached.

TROUBADOUR a traveling singer that emerged in the 11th to 13th centuries in France. In contrast to the religious music of the time, their songs often told stories about love.

TURNTABLE a revolving disc on a record player. Hip hop musicians often use two turntables at once.

VOCAL CORDS part of the throat that vibrates and produces sound when air from the lungs passes through it.

WALTZ a type of music, and dance, that became a craze in Europe in the late 18th century. It has three beats in a bar.

WIND INSTRUMENT an instrument played by blowing air through one or more tubes such as a flute, saxophone or trumpet.

When we were children, we listened to our parents' collections of records, cassettes or CDs and tuned in to the radio to try to find new music. When our parents were children, it was more or less the same for them. But in the last twenty years, the way we can find and enjoy music has changed completely! Now, you can listen to pretty much anything you can think of—mostly for free—through the Internet. It's an amazing time for music lovers and you lucky guys can explore a whole world of music from your own homes!* Sometimes, though, it can be tricky to know where to begin! First off, we've created an online playlist for each chapter in our book so you can listen to lots of the pieces we talk about by scanning the QR code on the right. You'll also find tracks on the playlist that we wanted to include in the book, but couldn't fit in the pages.

Scan this QR code to access the online playlist, or visit this web address: **https://sptfy. com/historyofmusic**

When you hear something you like the sound of, you can look up more pieces by the same composer or band. Music streaming services often include links to "other artists you might like" or an "artist radio" which puts together a collection of tracks from similar musicians.

Don't search the Internet without your adults' permission, but YouTube is another great place to discover performers—past and present. You'll find them playing live, talking about music or posing in videos. In one morning you could watch archive footage of electrifying performers like drummer Viola Smith in 1939, pianist Art Tatum in 1943; see The Beatles performing on the roof of Apple records in Soho, London in 1969; or watch Fela Kuti play the Berlin jazz festival in 1978. As well as searching for musicians, bands or composers, you can also search by piece, genre or instrument. You could find violin music by looking up "violin concerto," "klezmer fiddle" or by picking the name of a favourite violinist—like Itzhak Perlman or Nicola Benedetti.

There's a world of music out there. **HAPPY LISTENING!**

* Streaming is amazing for listeners, but it's not always so great for music makers as their tracks have to be streamed many millions of times before they can earn a living. Hopefully this will change in the coming years to be fairer to musicians!

SOURCES

In the course of writing this book and thinking about the musicians and music of the past, we've listened to hours of music, watched lots of documentaries and clips online and read many music books. Most of these are not aimed at children, but as they have informed our thinking we wanted to mention them here. They include:

BOOKS

Burrows, Terry. *The Art of Sound: A Visual History For Audiophiles.* London, New York, Melbourne: Thames & Hudson, 2017.

Byrne, David. *How Music Works.* San Francisco: McSweeney's, 2012. Edinburgh: Canongate, 2013.

Cooke, Mervyn. *The Chronicle of Jazz.* New York: Oxford University Press, 2013.

Gioia, Ted. *Music: A Subversive History.* New York: Basic Books, 2019.

Kureshi, Hanif and Jon Savage (eds.). *The Faber Book of Pop.* London: Faber & Faber, 1995.

Levitin, Daniel. *This Is Your Brain On Music.* Boston: Dutton Penguin, 2006; London: Grove/Atlantic, 2007.

Levitin, Daniel. *The World In Six Songs.* Boston: Dutton Penguin, 2008.

MacDonald, Ian. *Revolution in the Head: The Beatles' Records and the Sixties.* London: 4th Estate, 1994. Chicago: Chicago Review Press, 2007.

Piskor, Ed. *Hip Hop Family Tree 1975-1983 Vols. 1-2.* Seattle: Fantagraphics, 2014.

Ross, Alex. *Listen To This.* New York: Farrar, Straus and Giroux, 2010.

Ross, Alex. *The Rest Is Noise.* New York: Farrar, Straus and Giroux, 2007; London: 4th Estate, 2008.

Rusbridger, Alan. *Play It Again.* New York: Farrar, Straus and Giroux, 2013; London: Jonathan Cape, 2013.

Sacks, Oliver. *Musicophilia: Tales of Music and the Brain.* New York: Knopf, 2007; London: Picador, 2007.

Stanley, Bob. *Yeah Yeah Yeah: The Story of Modern Pop.* New York: W. W. Norton & Company, 2013.

Various authors. *Rough Guides to Music.* Rough Guides, 1999–

PODCASTS & WEBSITES

Grove Music Online. https://www.oxfordmusiconline.com/grovemusic/ [last accessed 30 November 2020]

Metropolitan Museum of Art, The. *Heilbrunn Timeline of Art History.* https://www.metmuseum.org/toah/ [last accessed 30 November 2020]

Song Exploder. Songexploder.net [last accessed 30 November 2020]

TV & FILM

Demme, Jonathan (dir.). *David Byrne, Stop Making Sense.* Arnold Stiefel Company, 1984.

Denselow, Robin (prod.). *Brasil Brasil.* BBC, 2017.

Evans, Guy (prod.). *Black Classical Music: The Forgotten History.* Douglas Road Productions, 2020.

Hanly, Francis (dir.). *Howard Goodall's Story of Music.* Tiger Aspect, 2013.

Luhrmann, Baz (dir.). *The Get Down.* Bazmark Films, Sony Pictures Television, 2016.

Tavernor, Clare (dir.). *Africa: A Journey Into Music.* Sundog Pictures Ltd, 2018.

Wasserman, Nico (dir.). *Stewart Copeland's Adventures in Music.* Somethin' Else, 2020.

LIST OF ILLUSTRATIONS

Dimensions are given in centimetres, followed by inches

INDEX

We'd like to thank Rose Blake for her inspiring and beautiful pictures; our wonderful children, Arlo, Zubin, Quincy & Viola, who managed to navigate the trials of home learning while we were writing this book in coronavirus lockdown; and all the brilliant children and parents who have played in the John Stainer Orchestra over the last few years. We'd like to dedicate this book to the thousands of talented musicians forced into hibernation in 2020. – M.R. & D.S.

I illustrated this book whilst going through a very stressful time in solo lockdown, so I'd like to thank Mary, David, Anna and Avni for being patient with me, it's been such a pleasure working with you all. Having the focus of drawing this book really helped me to get out of bed in the morning! Thanks to my friends for pulling me up when I've been a grump recently: Hannah, Paddy, Sophie, Ellie, Matthew, Nat, Narghi, Lucy, Maisie and the rest! And thank you to my Mum for teaching me the importance of music, harmony and singing out from day one. Also, thanks to Tara and Alexis for the secret chord! – R.B.

A History of Music for Children © 2021 Thames & Hudson Ltd, London

Text © 2021 Mary Richards and David Schweitzer
Illustrations © 2021 Rose Blake

Consultant Vinod Aithal

All Rights Reserved. No part of this publication may be reproduced or transmitted in any form or by any means, electronic or mechanical, including photocopy, recording or any other information storage and retrieval system, without prior permission in writing from the publisher.

First published in 2021 in the United States of America by Thames & Hudson Inc., 500 Fifth Avenue, New York, New York 10110

Reprinted 2022

Library of Congress Control Number 2021933959

ISBN 978-0-500-65247-3

Printed in China by Shanghai Offset Printing Products Limited

MIX
Paper from
responsible sources
FSC® C109093

Be the first to know about our new releases, exclusive content and author events by visiting
thamesandhudson.com
thamesandhudsonusa.com
thamesandhudson.com.au